Bridges
A Project Book

Dedicated to Stewart MacGregor,
the Builder, and Bern MacGregor,
the Believer

Bridges is designed to encourage children to
participate in the learning experience—to learn
by practical example. It traces the history of
bridge building throughout the world, but does
more than tell a story. It invites the reader to
take and use readily available materials to make
three different bridge models: an arch bridge, a
lifting bridge, and a suspension bridge.
Simple instructions, clearly illustrated, are
included and, as far as possible, are based on
real architectural and engineering principles.
Technical terms, translated into layman's
language, make this book interesting reading for
children and parents alike.

Bridges

A Project Book

Anne and Scott MacGregor

Lothrop, Lee & Shepard Books • New York

The Authors wish to thank the following organizations for assistance with information and materials for *Bridges*: The New South Wales Government Office; the United States Information Service; and the Cement and Concrete Association.

Designed by Nick Thirkell assisted by Ian Loveday

Library of Congress Cataloging in Publication Data
MacGregor, Anne, (date)
Bridges.
(A Project book for young people)
SUMMARY: Discusses the history, use, and construction of the three types of bridges. Includes instruction for making models and variations of each type.   1. Bridges—Juvenile literature.
[1. Bridges.]   I. MacGregor, Scott, (date)
joint author.   II. Title.   III. Series: Project book for young people.
TG148.M26   624′.2   80-23305
ISBN 0-688-41997-6 (pap.)   ISBN 0-688-51997-0 (lib. bdg.)

Contents

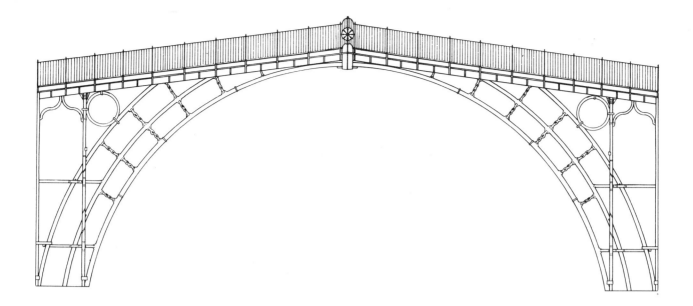

I The First Bridges

The first bridges were built for the same reason that bridges are built today—that is, to make life easier. When humans first walked across the open countryside, there were many obstacles barring their way. Sometimes one would have to walk for miles in order to avoid a wide, fast-flowing river or mountains that were too steep to climb. Such problems became worse when a family traveled with their belongings.

People built their shelters in places they could defend and in locations convenient for supplies of food and water. Rivers and streams often had to be crossed to get from place to place while hunting and gathering food.

Many of the earliest bridges were "invented" or suggested by natural happenings. A tree fallen across a stream could be walked over. Thick vines growing up between these trees were sometimes strong enough to carry animals swinging from tree to tree. Indeed, people probably copied this means of transportation to travel across forests and jungles. Also, stones carried by water would settle in shallow parts of a river or stream, providing yet another kind of walkway.

Fortunately for us, the human need to get about became so great that bridges made from these same, natural materials were created and have been developing ever since. Many mistakes have been made since the first bridges were built; however, almost every time a bridge has collapsed, another stronger and safer one has replaced it. The results are the magnificent bridges we see around us today.

Three Types

Even though man continues to find a better way of doing almost everything he's done before, he hasn't been able to find a better way of designing bridges. Beam, arch, and suspension bridge designs work so well, they don't need improvement. Changes in the appearance of bridges are a result of the use of new materials. The same basic ideas apply underneath all the concrete and steel that bridges are made of today.

The *beam* bridge is much like the tree that fell across the river. It is simple in design and may extend over long distances.

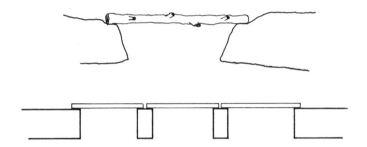

The *cantilever* is a type of beam bridge. Its span is counterbalanced for added strength so that such bridges can cover greater distances.

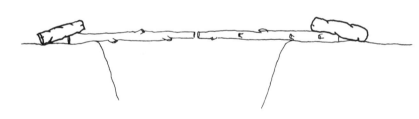

The *arch* bridge may have a curved or a flat deck. Its rounded or flattened curving arch is so designed to allow boats to pass underneath.

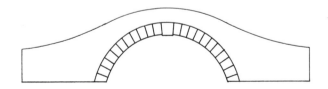

The *suspension* bridge is able to cross the widest valleys and waterways. Such bridges can be built so high that the largest ships are able to pass beneath them.

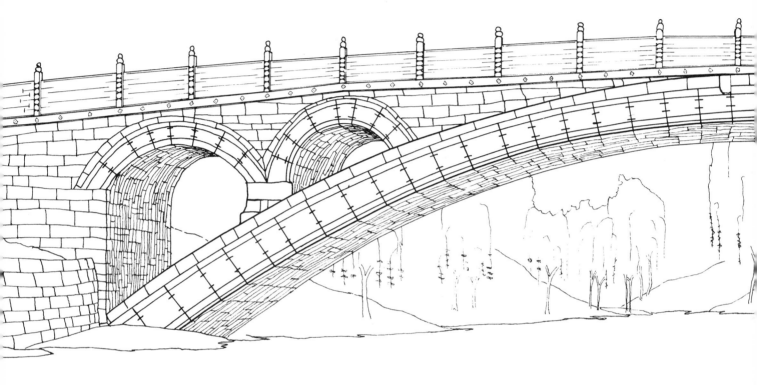

The first bridges were built thousands of years ago. They were made of materials that were easily found, such as stone, wood, and vines. The nature or type of bridges changed according to the needs of the people who built and used them.

The An-Chi Bridge at Chao Chou, China, is the oldest open-spandrel arch bridge in the world and is still in use today. Li Ch'un, who built the An-Chi around the year 600 A.D., designed his 36m (117-foot) bridge to be able to take great weights and therefore be strong enough to last many years. An interesting feature of this bridge, making it both beautiful to look at and particularly functional, is the arch-shaped openings in the *spandrels*, or walls, of the bridge.

During the rainy season in China, rivers would often flood and bridges were destroyed by the force of floodwaters. By making such openings in the walls of a bridge, floodwater could flow through it without causing damage.

Chinese builders also discovered how strong an arch could be without using more materials than were needed. The An-Chi is proof that a structure's real strength is its design, and not necessarily what it is made of. It is interesting to compare this bridge, which was built almost fourteen hundred years ago, with those now being erected. That arch bridges haven't changed proves that it is difficult to improve on a sound engineering principle.

The arch had been used merely as a decoration in buildings for two thousand years before the Europeans realized how useful it would be in bridge building. It was the practical Romans who eventually gave Europe the stone arch, and for the next eighteen hundred years this type of bridge was perhaps the most frequently built.

The first Roman bridges were made of wood, coated with *alum*, a chemical that made them fireproof. Such bridges were instrumental in helping the Roman army travel great distances, winning new lands for their empire. They had to be strong to withstand the weight of the troops wearing heavy armor and weapons; they had to be wide to enable troops to march in formation; and, most important, they had to be built quickly so that the legions could move with speed. Indeed, the success of the Roman legions may well have been a result of such bridges, which helped them move more easily than those whom they conquered.

After the Romans won their wars, they went about the job of building monuments to their heroes, temples and churches to their gods, and more permanent roads and bridges helping to establish trading routes throughout the empire.

A good example of the Roman way of doing things is the Pont du Gard (above), an aqueduct that was built in the year 14 A.D. at Nîmes, France. This bridge carries water from the Gard River 40km (25 miles) to the town of Nîmes. Water is so heavy that such aqueducts needed to be incredibly strong. Here, the strength came from a series of irregularly spaced arches built on three levels. The stones used in the construction were cut and fitted so perfectly that on the first two levels mortar was not used to hold them together. When the final tier was built, the aqueduct reached a majestic height of 47m (155 feet), which is as high as some of the suspension bridges being built today.

A building boom in Europe during the Middle Ages provided further opportunity for new bridge ideas and uses. Bridge designs contained chapels and resting places for travelers and defensive devices such as the iron gate *portcullis*, which could be lowered in event of attack. Built in 1260, the stone arch bridge at Monmouth, England, had such a portcullis. Though it has undergone some changes through the years, including widening at its approaches for motor traffic, its basic structure has remained the same.

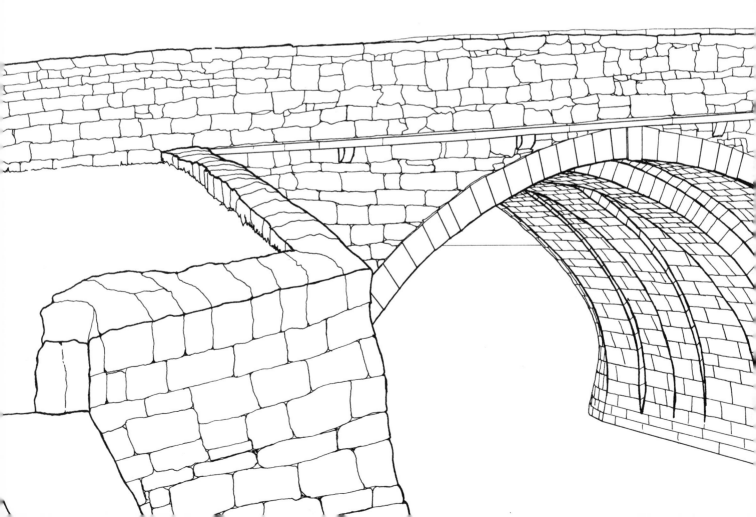

13

What There Is to Know about Arch Bridges

An arch bridge is a structure in *compression*. It gets its strength from the force exerted sideways, against its ends, or *abutments*. The first type of arch used in building was the false, or *corbeled*, arch.

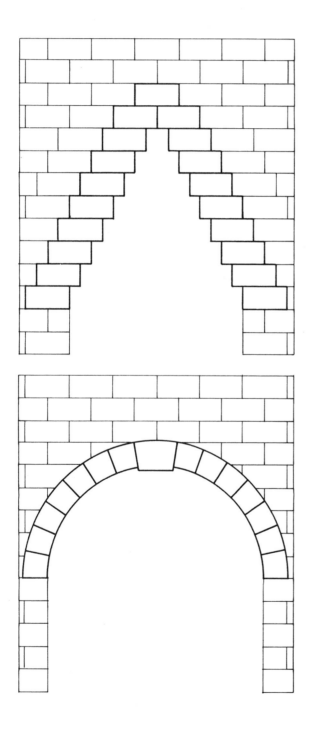

The *corbeled* arch (top left) resembled two sets of steps meeting in the middle. Bricks or stones were placed on top of each other, each layer projecting further than the one below it until the two sides met.

The arch was gradually refined until the true arch, or *voussoir*, (below left) was invented. Wedge-shaped stones or bricks were fitted together against abutments and *piers*, the vertical supports between two ends. Such an arch was built from its ends toward its middle, using a timber framework called *centering* or *falsework*.

The stones were laid over the framework until the final wedge, known as the *keystone*, was set in place at the crown of the bridge. Side walls, or spandrels, were built up between the arches, filled with rubble, and covered by a deck.

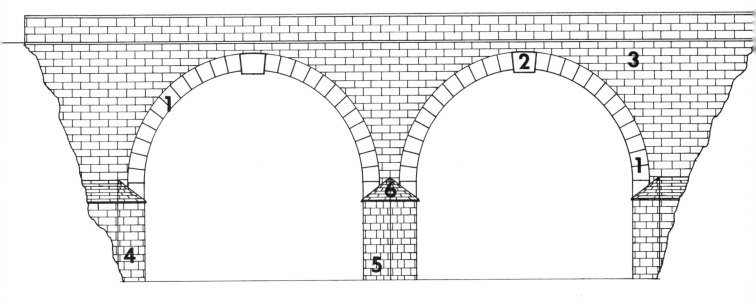

1. Voussoirs
2. Keystone
3. Spandrel
4. Abutment
5. Pier
6. Cutwater (Starling)

The power of moving water is so great that only bridges designed in consideration of this force have survived. The Romans built pointed *cutwaters*, or *starlings*, on the upstream side of their bridges. The downstream side featured squared cutwaters. As a result, many of their bridges suffered considerable damage by the Middle Ages. It was at this time that pointed downstream cutwaters were introduced into bridge design, and the damaged Roman bridges were rebuilt using this feature.

A further development during this period was the *ribbed* arch, which was made by using rows of wedge-shaped bricks or stones, independent of each other. Longer, flatter stones were laid across the rings, or ribs, to support interior stones or rubble infill. The new technique reduced the weight of the arch and cut construction time and materials. The Monmouth Bridge on pages 12–13 is a fine example of the rib-arch construction.

Build an Arch Bridge

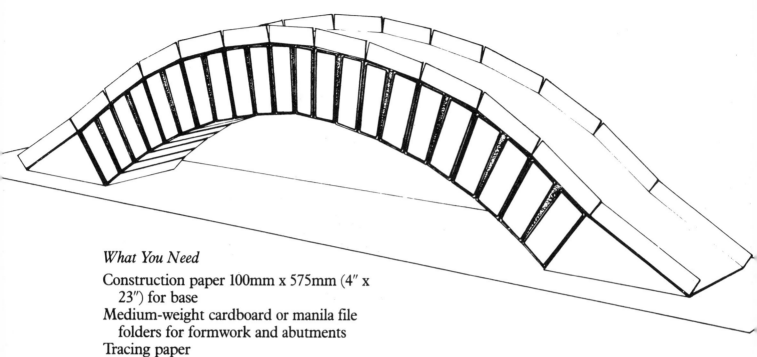

What You Need

Construction paper 100mm x 575mm (4″ x 23″) for base

Medium-weight cardboard or manila file folders for formwork and abutments

Tracing paper

22 matchboxes 52mm x 37mm x 17mm (2⅛″ x 1½″ x ¾″) or styrofoam strip at least 750mm (30″) long

11 wooden matchsticks 50mm (2″) long, points removed

Pencil, ruler, scissors, X-acto knife (if you use styrofoam), white glue (such as Elmer's Glue-All or Sobo)

Directions

1. With pencil, draw two parallel lines 365mm (14¼″) apart, at equal distances from both ends, on construction paper base strip.
2. Trace formwork pattern and transfer to medium-weight cardboard or file folder. Cut out.

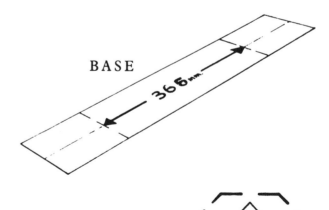

BASE

365mm

FORMWORK

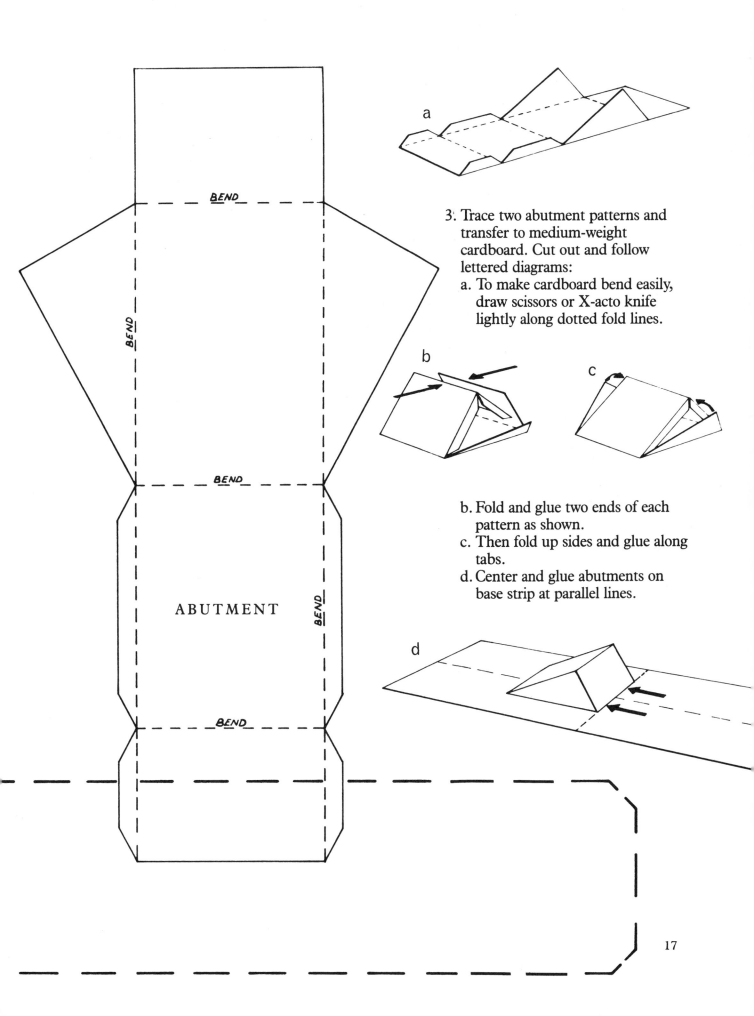

BEND

BEND

BEND

BEND

ABUTMENT

BEND

BEND

a

b

c

d

3. Trace two abutment patterns and transfer to medium-weight cardboard. Cut out and follow lettered diagrams:
a. To make cardboard bend easily, draw scissors or X-acto knife lightly along dotted fold lines.

b. Fold and glue two ends of each pattern as shown.
c. Then fold up sides and glue along tabs.
d. Center and glue abutments on base strip at parallel lines.

17

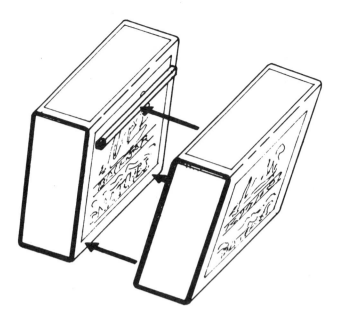

4. To make 11 voissoirs that form arch, glue one matchstick between two matchboxes as shown. Or you can cut voissoirs out of styrofoam, using pattern to the right and making each segment no longer than 50mm (2″) long. (If you use styrofoam, you will not need matchsticks.)

Assembly

5. Arch formwork and place between abutments. Building from both sides toward the center, place matchboxes along formwork until only the keystone is missing. Put in keystone and gently remove formwork. The pressure of the bridge units against each other will hold bridge together.

FOAM

VOISSOIR

Test It

To make sure your bridge works like an arch bridge, test it! You can see how strong the voissoir arch is by pressing anywhere along the arch. If you've made it properly, it won't collapse.

Use It

Don't let your bridge just sit there—use it! Glue all the matchboxes together along their sides and to the abutments. Cut out a strip of cardboard 560mm x 65mm (22″ x 2½″). This will be the deck. Turn up the side edge about 8mm (¼″) to make handrails; then glue the deck to the arch. Now you can drive toy cars, trucks, or even trains over it.

Variations

Don't be satisfied with your simple bridge. Add to the design to make it one that is truly your own. A tower or a gatehouse from your own pattern can be glued to the deck of the bridge. You can paint your bridge with poster paints too!

BRIDGE DECKING

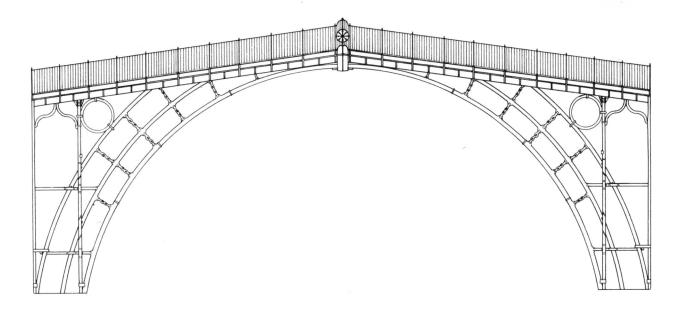

II The Age of Invention

Bridges became an important by-product of the Industrial Revolution, which began in Britain in the eighteenth century and extended to Europe and America soon after. The era was soon marked by great invention and scientific developments that provided opportunities for practical men to do great things.

In Britain there was a change from an agricultural economy to one of manufacturing. There was a shortage of land throughout the country and the lure of factory jobs in towns created a mass migration from rural areas. Factories produced goods needed by a rapidly expanding population—goods with which to fight wars, and those needed in peace time. Britain's trading routes were long established and her goods were wanted throughout the world. Industry thrived.

To support manufacturing, new transportation systems were devised. By 1750 the construction of a canal system enabled heavy cargo, such as coal and machinery, to be carried great distances. The width and depth of canalways varied so much that moving bridges, which could accommodate all kinds of traffic, were developed.

During the same period, experimentation resulted in the development of a method of economically producing iron in great quantities. Though the discovery of iron dates back to prehistoric times, it hadn't been used extensively.

The time was right for iron in the eighteenth-century world. In Europe, forests were fast running out of timber, and the need for speed in building to keep pace with the rapid developments of the industrial era prevented the further use of stone.

Coalbrookdale in Shropshire, England, has been called the "cradle" of the Industrial Revolution. Coal has been mined there since the sixteenth century, and factories and an iron foundry were firmly established by the mid-eighteenth century. In 1775 the town's businessmen commissioned architect Thomas Pritchard to design a bridge made of iron that would replace the town's ferry as well as create a demand for further iron constructions.

Abraham Darby III and John Wilkinson, the foundry's owners, altered the architect's design and the result is Iron Bridge, a single, semicircular arch, supported by five cast-iron ribs, with a span of 31m (100.5 feet) and a rise of 14m (45 feet). The 21m (70-foot) main ribs were cast in open sand molds, which was in itself a great achievement. Never before had iron been cast on so large a scale.

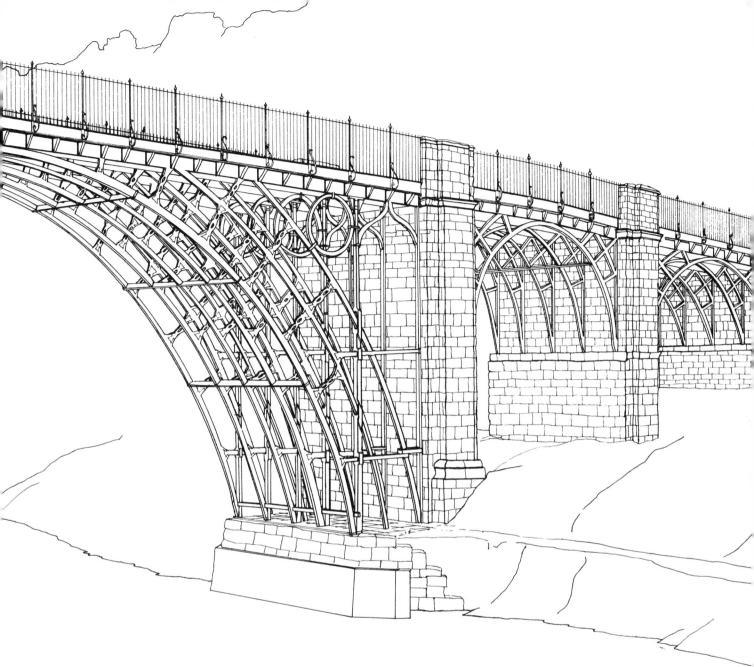

Because iron was a new material for bridge building, it was treated much like wood. Iron Bridge, which was completed in 1781, featured carpentry dovetails, shoulder joints, and wedge fittings. Amazingly, not a single bolt or rivet was needed to hold the pieces together.

Similarly, the abutments were taken from a stone arch design. The weight of an arch made of stone would have been sufficient to keep these abutments straight. However, the iron arch, being lighter, could not match the force being exerted on the abutments from earth pressure behind them, and this caused the bridge to rise at its center. The lesson was a good one, and the same mistake was avoided in future iron arch bridges.

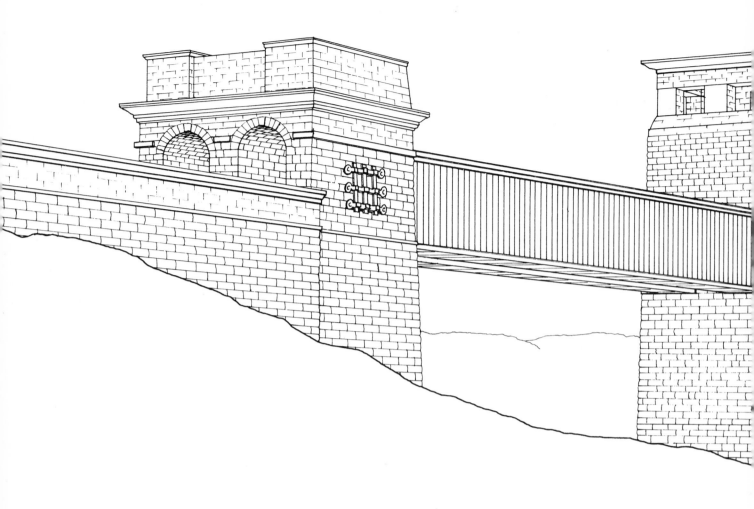

By the mid-nineteenth century, canal transport had been replaced by railroads. The Britannia Bridge was built by Robert Stephenson in 1850 to carry the Chester and Holyhead Railway over the Menai Straits in Wales. Its design provided a new and exciting use for iron—that is, as a box girder structure.

After three years of laboratory research, Stephenson, together with engineer/shipbuilder William Fairburn, devised a design using a series of four pairs of rectangular tubes or boxes. The side walls of the boxes were reinforced to prevent the boxes from wrinkling or twisting when a train passed through them.

The boxes were covered by wrought-iron plate and held together by no less than two million rivets. This construction technique was taken from the manufacture of ships, which at that time were similarly clad with iron plate.

The four pairs of tubes, laid parallel to each other, became a continuous girder, or beam, spanning 461m (1511 feet). Together they were stronger than separate girders, as each span had the effect of counterbalancing the span alongside it.

Stone towers were built to satisfy critics who didn't believe the tubes were strong enough to support themselves. The towers were built high enough to accommodate suspension chains, but Stephenson later proved that these were unnecessary.

Though this courageous design used a tremendous amount of material, costing at that time six hundred thousand British pounds, or three million U.S. dollars, the Britannia has had a great influence on bridge building right up to the present time.

In America, the *truss* was widely used in bridge building. If a wooden truss could hold up a roof, builders believed wooden trusses could be made strong enough to support bridges and the traffic that used them.

Unlike Britain, America had plenty of timber with which to build bridges, and many carpenters who could use their skills to construct those bridges. It was only natural that wooden trusses, which were inexpensive to build and easy and fast to construct, dominated American bridge building in the nineteenth century.

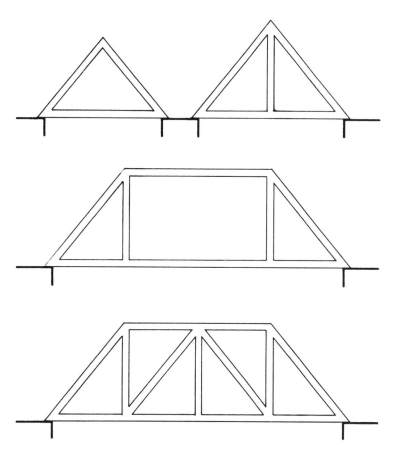

The truss design is based on the principle that a triangle cannot be twisted or distorted. By putting triangles next to each other, their strength becomes even greater.

Various combinations of triangles were tried in order to span greater distances.

The most common combination used a *king post*, the vertical support that results when two triangles share the same side.

The first truss design was patented in America in 1820, but at that time little was known or understood about what made it work. It wasn't until 1847, when the American Squire Whipple published his studies of trusses, that science was applied to this type of construction.

25

In the second half of the nineteenth century bridge traffic increased and loads became heavier. Wooden trusses had to be made stronger. The parts of a truss that would undergo stretching, or tension, were replaced by iron. First, cast iron was used, but this was later replaced by wrought iron. Cast iron was brittle; it wasn't flexible and would fracture when pulled. Though wrought iron was stronger, it unfortunately wasn't strong enough. During the 1870s forty bridges collapsed—that is, one in every four built in America during that time.

As a result, American companies began employing specialists. Carpenters could no longer build the more complicated bridges that were needed. Private firms of engineers specializing in bridge building were established, and standards were set for the future. Finally, cast iron was completely discarded as a material for bridge construction.

In 1879 the Tay Bridge in Scotland collapsed, killing all one hundred passengers traveling over it in a North British Railway train. This grand wrought-iron truss bridge had been weakened by frequent use, and the disaster occurred during a storm in which heavy winds weakened the trusses further. It was obvious that iron had outlived its usefulness and a new bridge material had to be found.

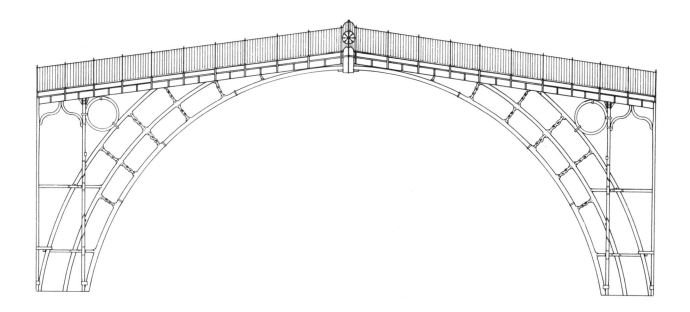

III Steel Bridges

Steel is a highly refined form of iron. The technique for making steel has been known in China since 200 B.C. and in Europe and Japan since the year 500 A.D. Nevertheless, it was so expensive to make in quantity that until the nineteenth century its use was strictly limited to the manufacture of small weapons, farm implements, and tools.

In 1857, American inventor William Kelly patented a series of designs for machines that would make steel cheaply. Kelly had little success in convincing people that steel could be made economically. He himself went bankrupt and was forced to discontinue his work. In the meantime, British inventor Henry Bessemer carried Kelly's discoveries further, developing a steel-making technique that to this day bears his name. Steel was resilient, more flexible than iron, and could be cut. By the 1870s steel was widely used in bridge building, and bridge design became more exciting than ever. So far no better material has been found to replace it.

In 1890 the Firth of Forth Railway Bridge was completed in Scotland (see overleaf). This most spectacular of bridges, spanning 2529m (8296 feet), used 59,055 tonnes (58,000 tons) of steel in its construction. Its *cantilevered truss* design was built for maximum stability. It used more materials than were necessary, as the memory of the Tay Bridge disaster was still fresh in everyone's minds.

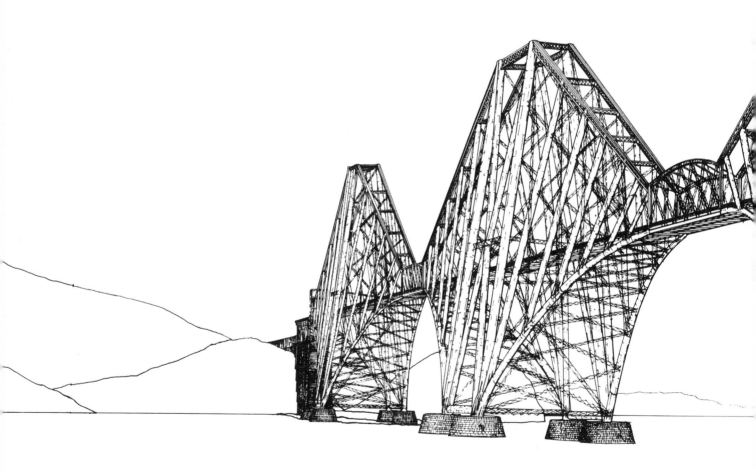

Tower Bridge, gateway to the busy port of London, was completed in 1894. Its design called for two lifting *bascules*, which enabled large ships to pass through the bridge's opening and navigate to London docks up the deep channel of the Thames.

The bridge's movable steel bascules each weigh 1120 tonnes (1100 tons), yet they can be lifted in a mere four minutes with the aid of hydraulic equipment that is built into the bridge's piers.

The decorative towers were made to look like the nearby Tower of London, but they have a real function in providing the operator of the bascules with a clear view of all angles of the bridge, the roadway, and the river. Such "lifting bridges" were inspired by the medieval drawbridge. Using the new, stronger materials in the nineteenth and twentieth centuries, they performed efficiently, eliminating transportation problems within cities where bridges couldn't always be built high enough for large ships to pass beneath them.

Steel proved how adaptable it could be as it continued to be used for new and exciting shapes in different bridge designs. The construction of bridges made from steel also changed from what builders were used to because the new material was easier to work with, as well as being far stronger than iron.

During its construction, the steel arch of the Sydney Harbour Bridge was cantilevered and supported on each side by 128 steel cables, which were anchored out from shore. In this way, no centering or falsework had to be used as was the case in early arch bridges.

Spanning 503m (1650 feet) across Australia's busiest harbor, shipping traffic was not restricted, as indeed it would have been by the falsework, throughout the seven years it took to build the bridge.

When the arch was completed, cables were hung as a means of support for the bridge's deck, which carried eight lanes of road traffic, four railway tracks, and two footpaths. Completed in 1932, the Sydney Harbour Bridge still holds the world's record for the heaviest load.

What There Is to Know about Moving Bridges

When we think of bridges, we think of structures that enable people to move more easily from one place to another. In the case of moving bridges, such structures must themselves move in order for people to get from one point to another.

There are four types of moving bridges. All owe their continued development to the introduction of steel.

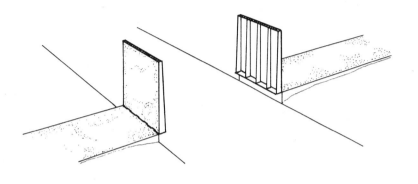

The *bascule*, like London's Tower Bridge (see pages 30–31), has decks that are lifted up from their ends.

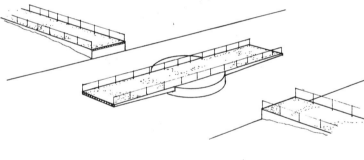

The *swing* bridge was first designed for use as a military bridge. It pivots out of the way.

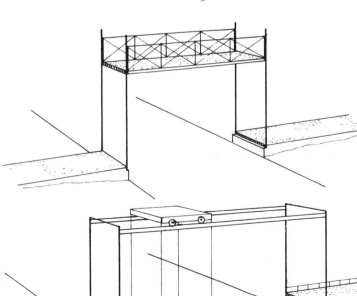

The *vertical lift* bridge was designed in the nineteenth century by Squire Whipple. Such bridges, in which the whole span is raised up, were first used over canals in upper New York State.

The *transporter* bridge ferries a moving platform that is suspended from a high-level horizontal track.

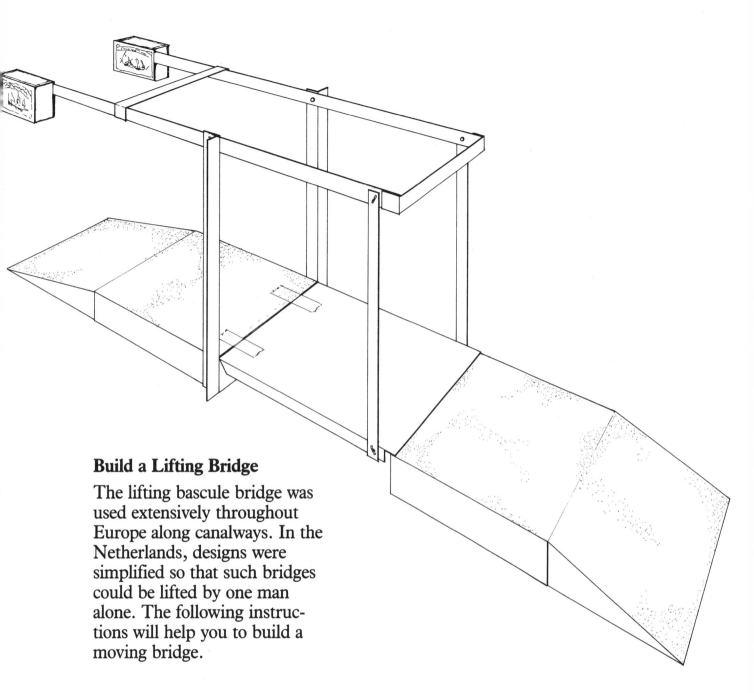

Build a Lifting Bridge

The lifting bascule bridge was used extensively throughout Europe along canalways. In the Netherlands, designs were simplified so that such bridges could be lifted by one man alone. The following instructions will help you to build a moving bridge.

What You Need

Medium-weight cardboard or manila file folders
Heavyweight cardboard or balsa wood 3mm
    (⅛″) thick, at least 320mm (12½″) long
Tracing paper
2 empty matchboxes
6 paper fasteners
Small pebbles or modeling clay
Pencil, ruler, scissors, X-acto knife (if you
    use balsa wood), white glue (such as
    Elmer's Glue-All or Sobo), cellophane tape

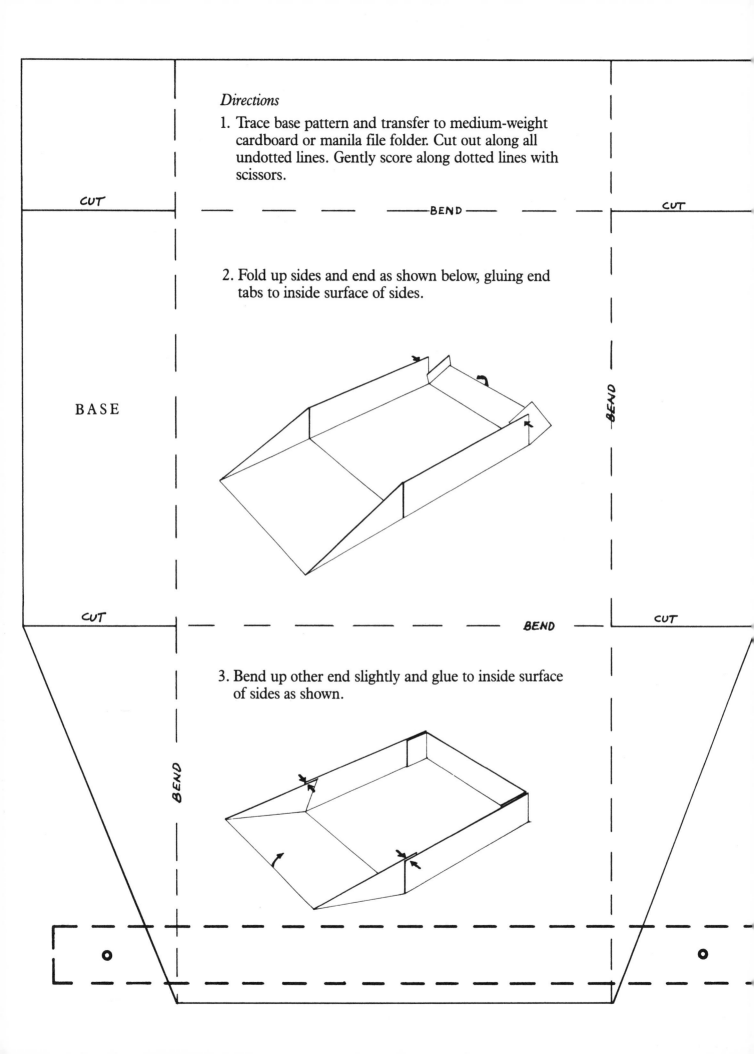

CUT

CUT

BEND

Directions

1. Trace base pattern and transfer to medium-weight cardboard or manila file folder. Cut out along all undotted lines. Gently score along dotted lines with scissors.

2. Fold up sides and end as shown below, gluing end tabs to inside surface of sides.

BASE

BEND

CUT

CUT

BEND

3. Bend up other end slightly and glue to inside surface of sides as shown.

BEND

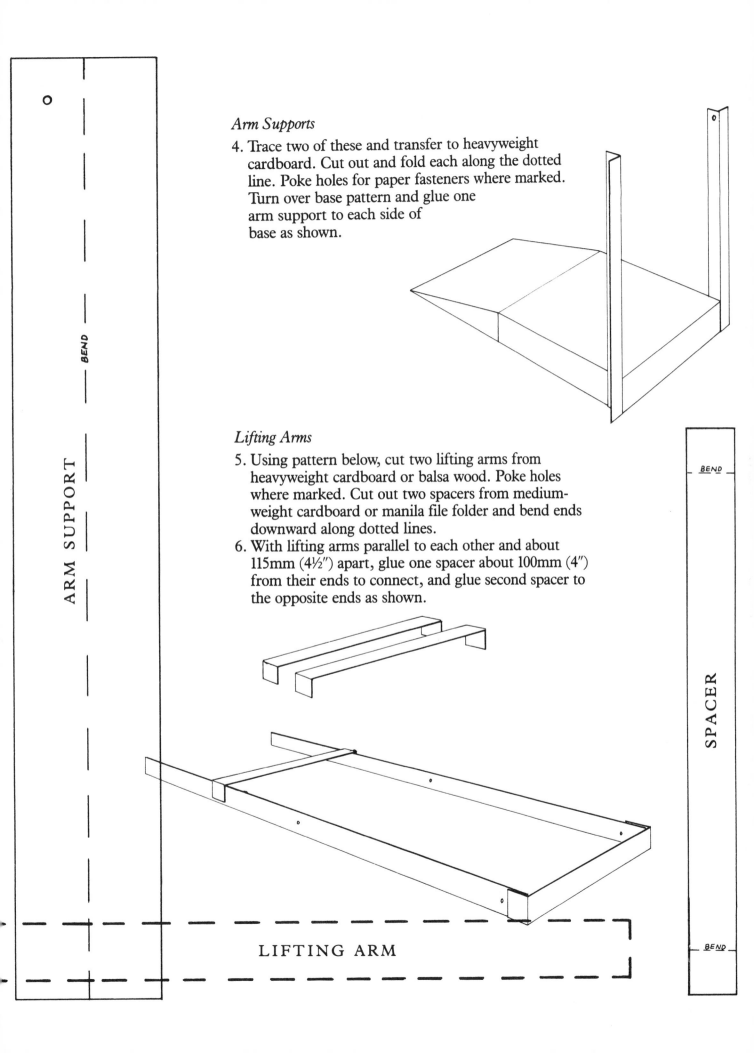

Arm Supports

4. Trace two of these and transfer to heavyweight cardboard. Cut out and fold each along the dotted line. Poke holes for paper fasteners where marked. Turn over base pattern and glue one arm support to each side of base as shown.

Lifting Arms

5. Using pattern below, cut two lifting arms from heavyweight cardboard or balsa wood. Poke holes where marked. Cut out two spacers from medium-weight cardboard or manila file folder and bend ends downward along dotted lines.

6. With lifting arms parallel to each other and about 115mm (4½″) apart, glue one spacer about 100mm (4″) from their ends to connect, and glue second spacer to the opposite ends as shown.

ARM SUPPORT

BEND

SPACER

BEND

BEND

LIFTING ARM

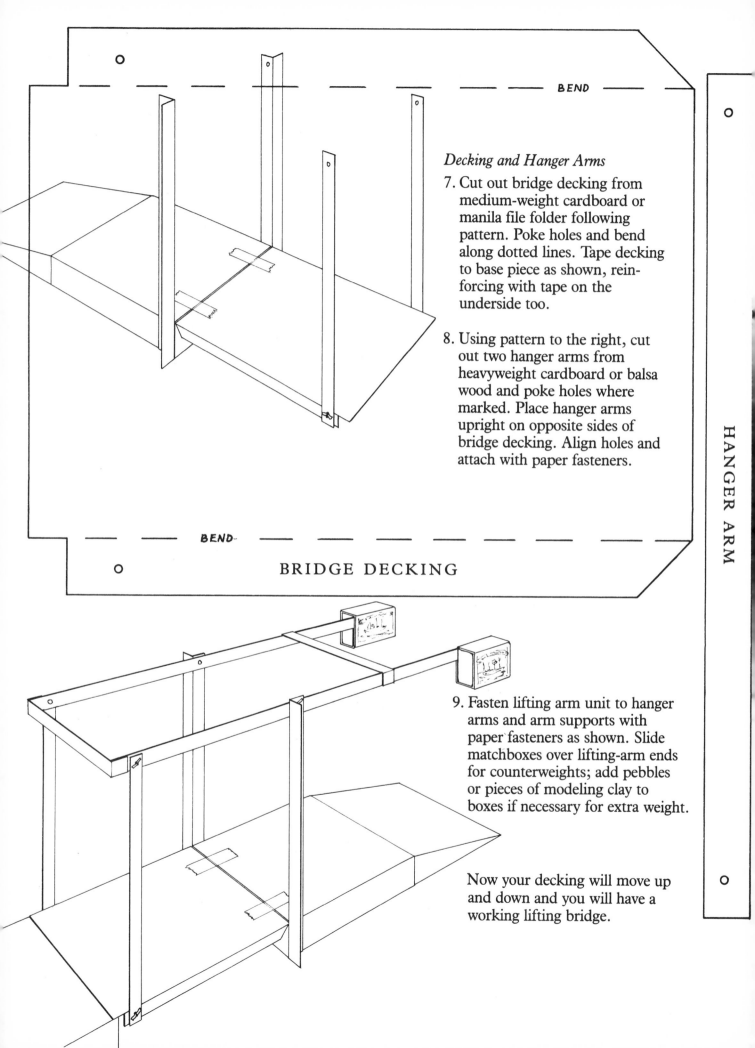

BEND

Decking and Hanger Arms

7. Cut out bridge decking from medium-weight cardboard or manila file folder following pattern. Poke holes and bend along dotted lines. Tape decking to base piece as shown, reinforcing with tape on the underside too.

8. Using pattern to the right, cut out two hanger arms from heavyweight cardboard or balsa wood and poke holes where marked. Place hanger arms upright on opposite sides of bridge decking. Align holes and attach with paper fasteners.

BEND

BRIDGE DECKING

HANGER ARM

9. Fasten lifting arm unit to hanger arms and arm supports with paper fasteners as shown. Slide matchboxes over lifting-arm ends for counterweights; add pebbles or pieces of modeling clay to boxes if necessary for extra weight.

Now your decking will move up and down and you will have a working lifting bridge.

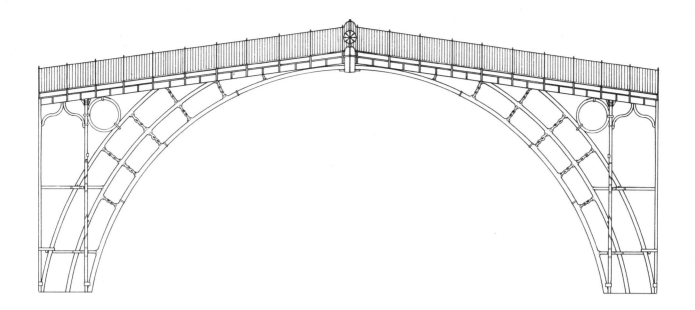

IV Suspension Bridges

The twentieth-century suspension bridge is a product of improved materials and highly developed building methods. Insofar as it is possible for a man-made structure to be in harmony with nature, such bridges do fit into their surroundings while at the same time serving a useful purpose.

Suspension bridges are capable of spanning the greatest distances with what appears to be a minimum of material. In fact, the suspension bridge, which is a tension structure, makes the most efficient use of the materials it uses. The result is a bridge with a graceful, delicate appearance, and at the same time a feeling of strength.

Regardless of their length, suspension bridges keep their character. Years after their construction, additional decks may be added to handle ever-increasing amounts of road and rail traffic.

Suspension bridge projects do not end at the banks of the waterways and open spaces they connect. Along with the development of suspension bridges are the highly complicated road systems that lead into them.

Because land for these roads is usually limited, roadways may cross under and over each other to allow a smooth flow of traffic. In such situations, all kinds of bridges are used to carry roadways. Beam bridges and sometimes arch bridges, made of reinforced concrete, become an important part of the suspension bridge project.

This footbridge over the River Min in the Szechwan Province of China was built during this century. Spanning 549m (1800 feet), it was designed in the style of the earliest suspension bridges. Cables or ropes are made from woven split bamboo. Wooden poles used for towers are protected from the weather by shingled roofs.

The Chinese developed iron-cable suspension bridges before the seventh century. However, the use of natural materials after that time may well have been because of economic necessity and an abundance of natural resources. This type of tension structure made the most efficient use of its materials, and the skills of its builders.

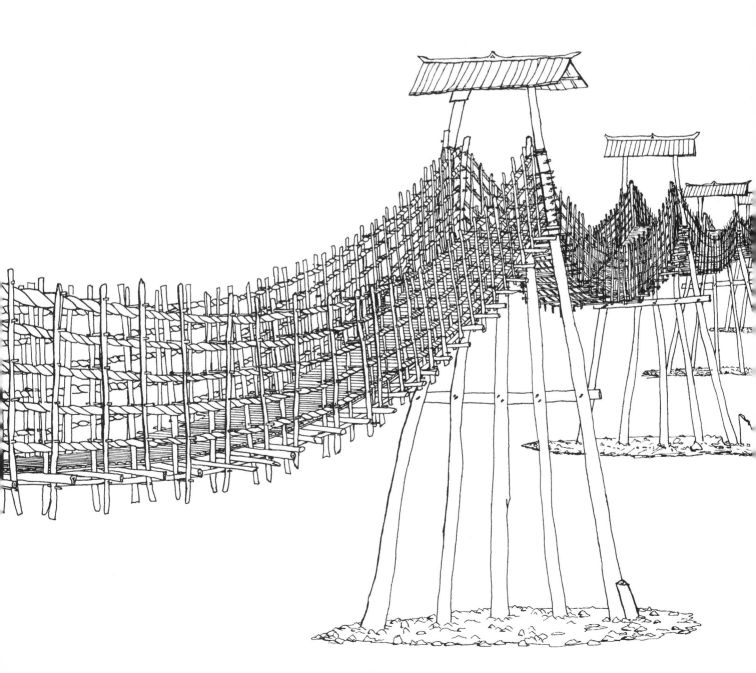

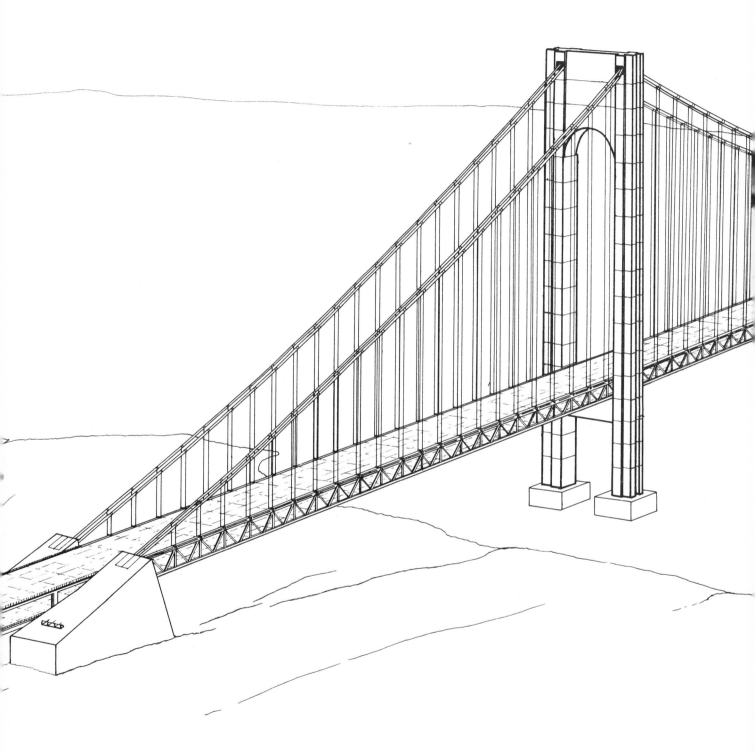

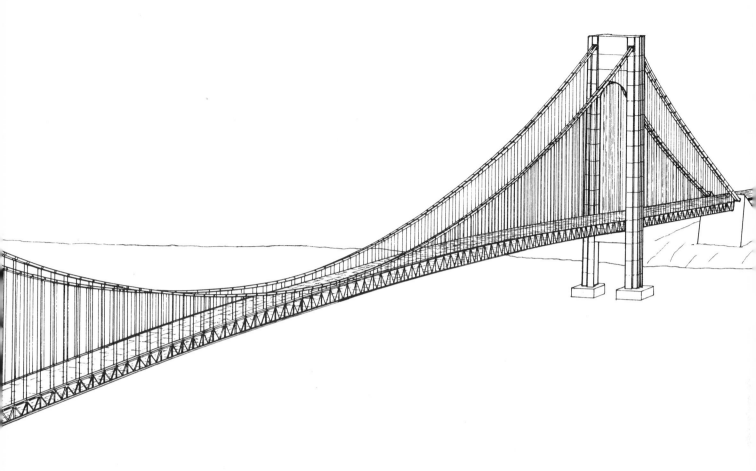

The Verrazano-Narrows Bridge connects New York's borough of Brooklyn with Staten Island. It took seventy years to plan and six years to build. When it was completed in 1965 it was said to be the bridge to end all bridges. As we've learned from history, there will always be another bridge that's bigger and better; but this one, designed by Othmar Ammann, who was also responsible for the George Washington Bridge, is still a spectacular achievement.

At 1299m (4260 feet), it is the world's longest suspension bridge. It is so long, in fact, that the curve of the earth's surface had to be taken into consideration in its design and construction. Though the towers are perfectly vertical, they are almost 51mm (2 inches) further apart at the top than they are at the base. When Britain's Humber Bridge is completed in the near future, it will be the result of improved construction methods and will, for a time, be the world's greatest.

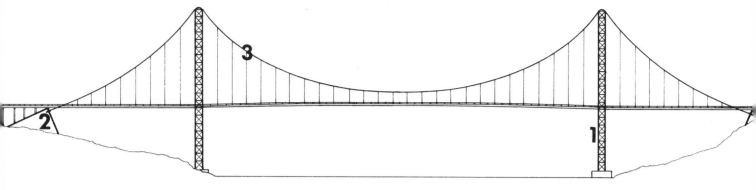

What There Is to Know about Suspension Bridges

The three most important parts of the suspension bridge are the *towers*, the *anchorages*, and the *cables*.

1. Towers have been made of wood, stone, and steel. Their height depends on the amount of sag, or curve, required for the cables.

2. The anchorages hold the ends of the cables and therefore must be strong. Usually they are set in stone or concrete if they cannot be fixed to natural rock.

3. The cables are the most important part of the bridge, as they support the roadway and give the bridge its shape and character. The first suspension bridges used cables made of vines and split bamboo woven into ropes. Modern suspension bridges use steel wire for maximum strength.

How Suspension Bridges Are Made

Concrete piers are built to support the bridge's towers. This may require the construction of *caissons*, which are underwater work chambers. Once the towers are fixed, the most important stage of construction begins—that is, the laying of the cables.

A connection must be made between the two banks. In prehistoric times, the first thread of a cable was fastened to an arrow and shot from one bank across to the other. Today wires can be transported by tugboats and hoisted into position. The first wires are set as a guide to determine the shape the cables will take. A footbridge or working platform is then built to enable all further work.

The *traveling rope*, which is an endless wire rope suspended over the river, is driven back and forth by machinery to draw the wires for the cable. After 250 to 450 wires have been drawn, they are tied at intervals to form a strong rope. *Hydraulic squeezers* press the wires together and these are strapped and covered by a continuous wrapping of wire for extra protection.

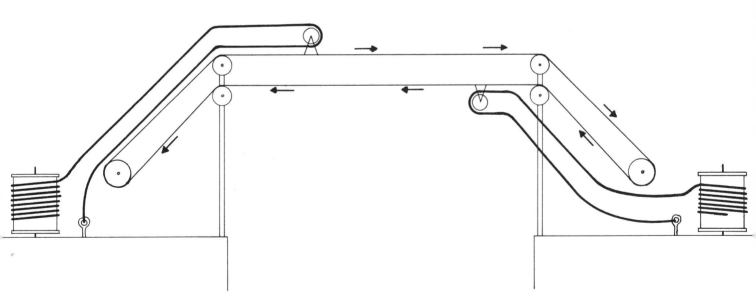

After all the cables are in place, suspenders are hung and the deck and its stiffening supports are constructed.

The suspension bridge's greatest enemy is wind, especially now that such bridges are becoming longer and lighter in weight. It's not so much how strong a wind may be, but the combination of its force and the direction it takes. A strong, steady wind can do less damage than lighter gusts coming from several directions at once. Because of the severe effect of wind on suspension bridges, they must be designed for safety in all sorts of weather.

In modern suspension bridges, the decking is designed to give stability to the entire structure. To do this effectively, box girders are replacing trusses as stiffening supports. They use less material, which makes the bridge lighter. Towers and anchorages don't need as much strength, so less material is used in these parts, too, giving the bridge a more streamlined appearance.

Decking and girders can be prefabricated—made in a factory and hoisted into place from the river below. This method saves builders both time and money. The decking, too, then takes on a new shape, more like that of the body of an aircraft. Wind moves freely around the deck and the stability of the entire structure is achieved.

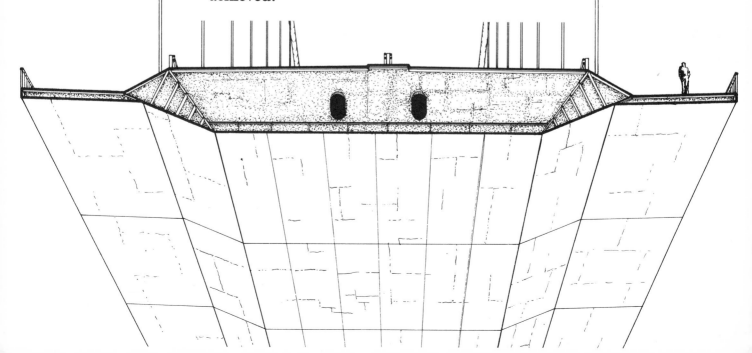

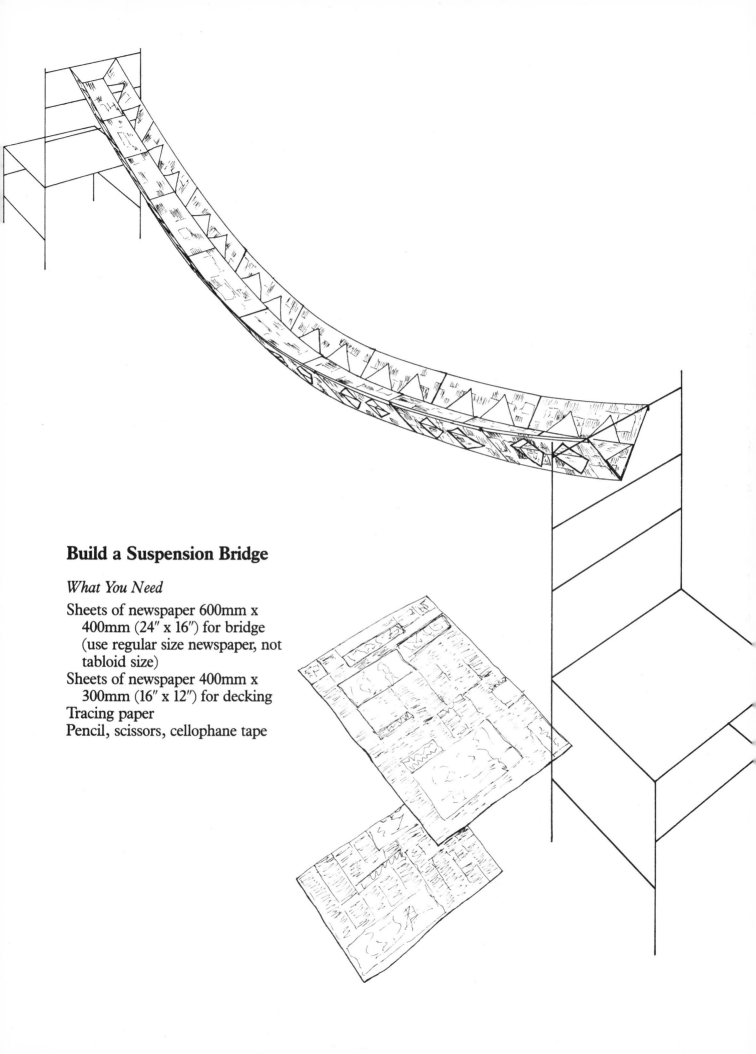

Build a Suspension Bridge

What You Need

Sheets of newspaper 600mm x
400mm (24″ x 16″) for bridge
(use regular size newspaper, not
tabloid size)
Sheets of newspaper 400mm x
300mm (16″ x 12″) for decking
Tracing paper
Pencil, scissors, cellophane tape

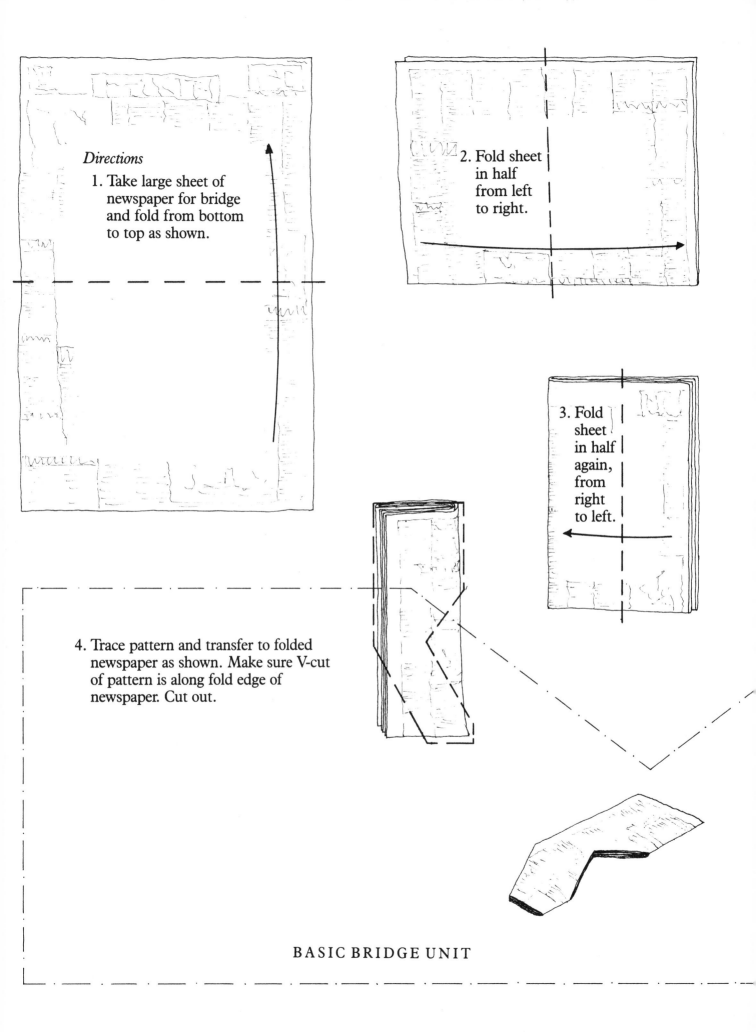

Directions

1. Take large sheet of newspaper for bridge and fold from bottom to top as shown.

2. Fold sheet in half from left to right.

3. Fold sheet in half again, from right to left.

4. Trace pattern and transfer to folded newspaper as shown. Make sure V-cut of pattern is along fold edge of newspaper. Cut out.

BASIC BRIDGE UNIT

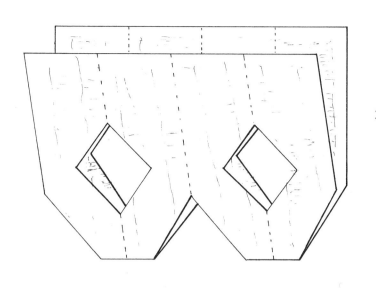

5. Open newspaper until there is only one fold left at bottom.

6. Along top, uncut edges, draw three 25mm (1″) bands. Fold bands accordion-style as shown in diagram. This is the basic bridge unit. Make at least ten of these.

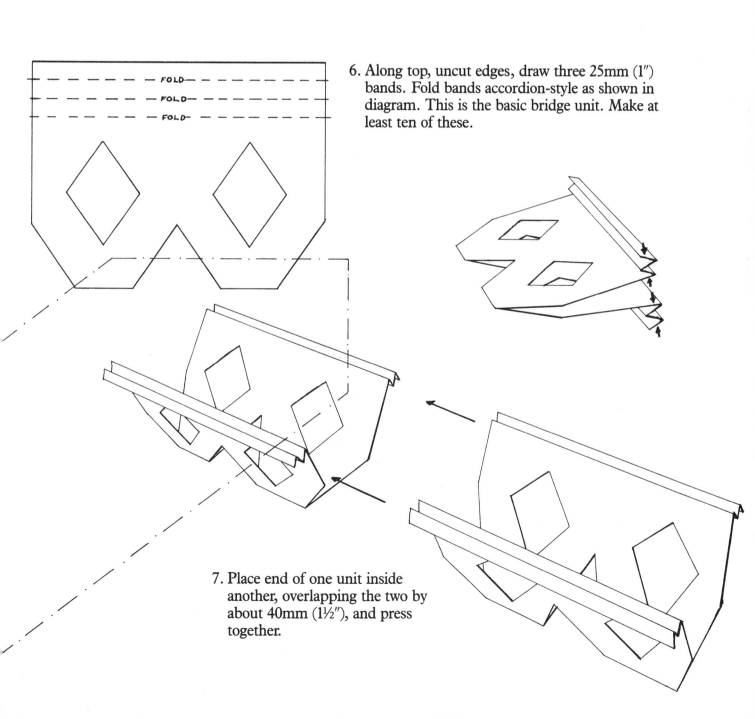

FOLD

FOLD

FOLD

7. Place end of one unit inside another, overlapping the two by about 40mm (1½″), and press together.

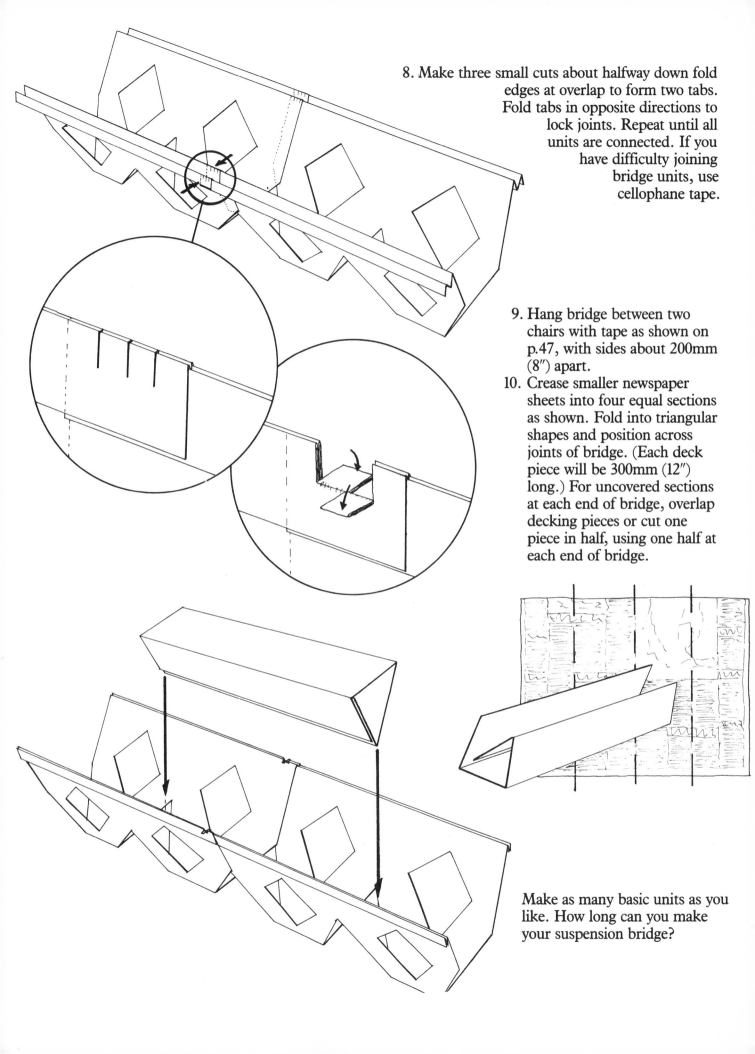

8. Make three small cuts about halfway down fold edges at overlap to form two tabs. Fold tabs in opposite directions to lock joints. Repeat until all units are connected. If you have difficulty joining bridge units, use cellophane tape.

9. Hang bridge between two chairs with tape as shown on p.47, with sides about 200mm (8″) apart.

10. Crease smaller newspaper sheets into four equal sections as shown. Fold into triangular shapes and position across joints of bridge. (Each deck piece will be 300mm (12″) long.) For uncovered sections at each end of bridge, overlap decking pieces or cut one piece in half, using one half at each end of bridge.

Make as many basic units as you like. How long can you make your suspension bridge?

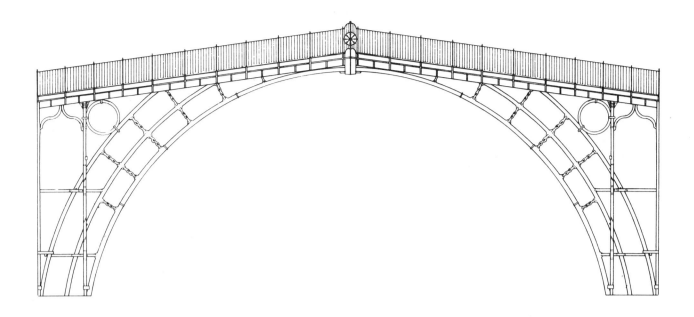

V Bridges for Today

The introduction and development of concrete gave bridge building a boost. In Europe, where raw materials were in short supply and skilled labor plentiful and relatively inexpensive, concrete became a popular material for bridge building.

Experiments in concrete were carried out throughout Europe, particularly in the industrialized countries of Britain, France, and Germany. In 1867 Joseph Monier, a French gardener and inventor, found a way of making anything from concrete flower pots to concrete bridges stronger. The way he strengthened concrete was to reinforce it with wire mesh. Monier was not an engineer by profession and his experiments were limited to small-scale projects. However, he conceived of an idea that was to be developed far beyond his dreams—one that was destined to become vital to future bridge building.

Monier's countryman Eugène Freyssinet continued the search for improvements to concrete. In 1904 he developed *pre-stressed* concrete, which is used in bridge building today, and he then designed a series of bridges (see page 56) that put the new material to good use.

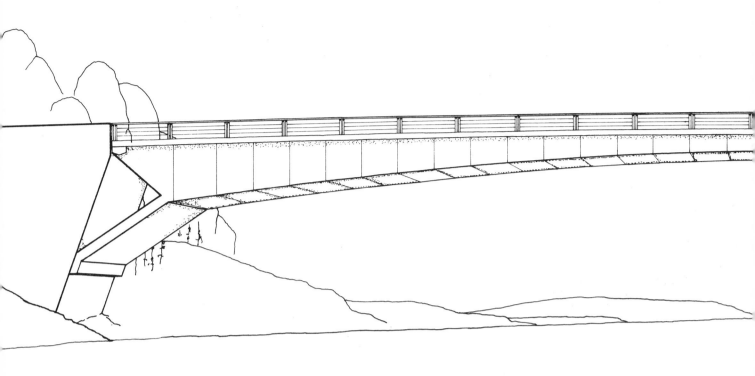

Concrete is made up of sand, small stones or man-made substitutes, and cement. It is a material that is very strong in compression. As a result, most of the first concrete bridges used an arch design, which in itself is strong in compression.

To use concrete in longer bridges and in bridges of different design, the material had to be strengthened against the forces of tension. It was found that by adding steel, which is strong in tension, to concrete, which is strong in compression, the resulting material would be stronger, more versatile, and less expensive than either material on its own.

Freyssinet created pre-stressed concrete using what is known as a *wet* and a *dry* technique. In the first, metal rods could be laced through concrete while it was still wet. Rods or cables would be held in tension during the drying and *curing*, or aging, process.

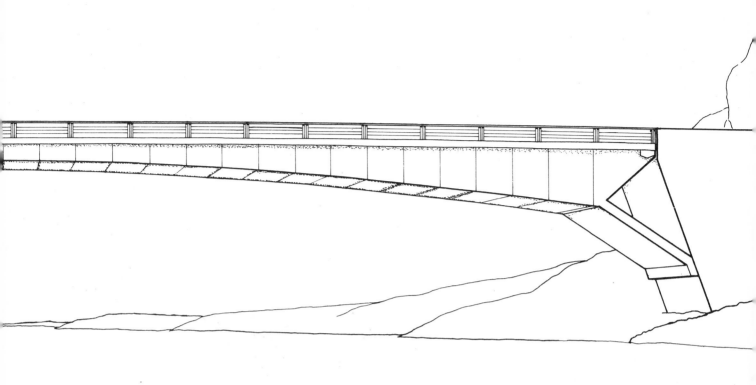

In the second technique, concrete could be cast in molds that would have holes or ducts through them. After the concrete was cured, cables or rods could be inserted and stretched for tensioning. The outside holes could later be sealed.

As improvements were made to concrete, construction methods changed. Parts of bridges such as voussoirs could be mass-produced in factories. Manufacturing these on a large scale reduced costs, saved time, and guaranteed uniform quality.

Voussoirs could be cast as hollow boxes to use the minimum of material. They would be assembled on site, using a simple scaffolding and falsework. Cemented together and reinforced by steel cable, they produced a finished product that looked good and took less time and money to build.

Concrete was a new material for twentieth-century builders. At the same time, it could be made to look like a more familiar material: stone. As a result, many early concrete bridges were faced with stone and designed in cumbersome shapes to give an appearance of being something they were not. However, Swiss designer of the thirties Robert Maillart, and those who followed him, appreciated the new material and realized that with its lightweight strength it could be used in more elegant and streamlined shapes.

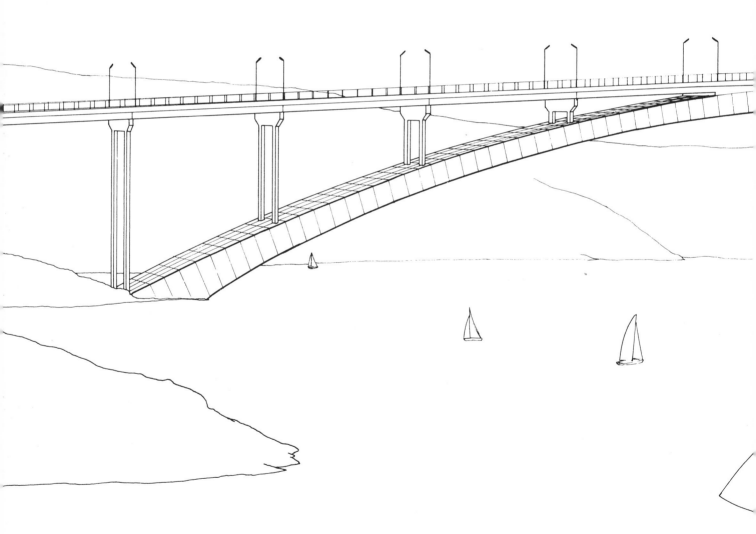

Australia's Gladesville Bridge, completed in 1964, is a result of hundreds of years of bridge building. Its main arch, spanning 305m (1000 feet), is made from hollow concrete voussoirs, a successful combination of twentieth-century technology and early Roman design. The voussoirs were manufactured in a factory and hoisted onto a steel falsework that also borrowed its design from history.

The Gladesville Bridge is a perfect example of man's need to better himself by borrowing from the efforts and experience of all who went before him. Fortunately, many early bridges were built strong enough to be with us even today. Despite the fact that their existence may be taken for granted in our high-speed world, they beautify the countryside and put us in touch with the past. They are also a convenience that centuries of people could not have survived without.